HELLO KITTY
Annual 2013

© 1976, 2012 SANRIO CO., LTD.

ISBN: 978-0-00-748572-7

1

Text by Kirsty Neale

First published in the UK by HarperCollins Children's Books in 2012

Printed and bound in China.

HarperCollins *Children's Books*

Welcome to my Annual for 2013!
It's packed with all sorts of things to keep you busy during the year. There are puzzles and quizzes, style ideas, things to make, lists to write and even parties to plan. I've also included plenty of tips and a few sneaky peeks into my exciting life. It's been lots of fun gathering everything together, and I hope you're going to love it all as much as I do. I've got a feeling 2013 is going to be a truly fabulous year! With lots of love,

Hello Kitty
XX

Contents

Hello Kitty's 13 for 2013!

This is a page all about me! I've made a list of thirteen things I want to do in 2013, and thirteen things I really love.

Thirteen things I want to do in 2013

- ✓ 1. Visit a city I've never been to before.
- ✓ 2. Write a special song with my band.
- ✓ 3. Try out a new fashion look.
- ✓ 4. Join a girls' football team.
- ✓ 5. Throw a fancy tea party.
- ✓ 6. Make breakfast in bed for Mama and Papa.
- ✓ 7. Go to the beach.
- ✓ 8. Learn how to squeeze yummy fresh fruit juice.
- ✓ 9. Get together with my friends for a fun photoshoot.
- ✓ 10. Make up a dance routine.
- ✓ 11. Send lots of letters to my penpal.
- ✓ 12. Invent a brand new recipe.
- ✓ 13. Make birthday cards for all of my friends instead of buying them.

Hello Kitty x x

Thirteen things I love

1. My friends and family
I love them all!

5. Shopping for cute clothes
How do I look?

9. London (my home town)
It's the greatest city in the world.

2. Taking photographs
Say cheese!

3. Playing and singing with my band
We totally rock!

4. Parties (especially sleepovers)
Who wants to play pass the parcel?

6. Baking tasty treats
Mama's apple pie is my favourite!

7. Anything sparkly
I'm a glitter-bug!

8. Going for bike rides
It's even more fun when Mimmy comes along.

12. Dressing up
Costumes are the coolest!

10. Drawing and painting
What shall I paint?

11. Reading
I love stories!

13. Going on holiday
I love to see new places.

My 13 for 2013

Now it's your turn! Write your own lists here and add some pictures, too.

Thirteen things I want to do in 2013

1.

2.

3.

4.

5.

6.

7.

8.

9.

10.

11.

12.

13.

Thirteen things I love

1. ....
2. ....
3. ....
4. ....
5. ....
6. ....
7. ....
8. ....
9. ....
10. ....
11. ....
12. ....
13. ....

Stick a picture here.
It can be a drawing or a photo.

Get doodling! Draw one of the things you love here.

Make a drawing of something on your list, or take a photo of someone you love, then stick it here.

This is a place for you to add a drawing or photo. Stick it down!

What's your favourite season?

Are you a winter wonder, full of the joys of spring, or do you prefer summer or autumn? Try this fun quiz and find out!

1. What do you usually have for lunch?
a) An enormous salad and a box of juicy raisins.
b) Crunchy crackers and a tasty yoghurt.
c) A pasta salad and a scrummy cupcake.
d) A chunky sandwich and some fresh fruit.

2. Your favourite outfit is:
a) Fun and fashionable.
b) Stylish and unique.
c) Warm and cosy.
d) Cute and comfortable.

3. What's your dream job?
a) A teacher.
b) An author.
c) A vet.
d) An explorer.

4. You really like stories about:
a) Holidays.
b) Magic.
c) Animals.
d) Adventure.

5. Where would you most like to go on holiday?
a) A beautiful, tropical beach.
b) A big city, like Paris or New York.
c) A ski resort with cosy chalets.
d) A huge theme park with lots to do.

Results

Mostly a)s: SUMMER
You're lively, honest, fun-loving and a total chatterbox. You love to party and your sunny nature means you're always the centre of attention.

Mostly b)s: AUTUMN
You're hardworking and super-smart, with a brilliant sense of humour. You love reading and listening to music and you're cooler than a chilly autumn day.

Mostly c)s: WINTER
You're kind, sweet, giggly and a really good friend. You love cute and cuddly animals, and throw the cosiest sleepovers in the world.

Mostly d)s: SPRING
You're enthusiastic, sporty and cheerful with bags of energy. You love spending time outdoors in the fresh spring air, and you're the green queen of recycling.

How to draw Hello Kitty

I love drawing and painting, especially pictures of all my friends. When I first started, it was really tricky, but then Papa showed me how to break down drawings into a few simple shapes. It's a brilliant idea, and it really works! Try it for yourself, and see if you can draw me. Do all of your preparation work with a pencil, then use a pen to trace round the edges.

1. Start by drawing an oval shape for my head.

2. Add two triangles for ears. Give them curvy points, instead of sharp ones.

3. Draw a wedge shape (like a slice of pizza) overlapping the oval.

4. Make my legs by adding a sideways 'B' at the bottom.

5. Draw a curve at either side to give me arms. Add two tiny semi-circles for thumbs.

6. Now I need my trusty bow! Draw a sideways figure '8' over my ear. Add a circle in the middle.

7. Draw an extra half-circle on each side of my hair-bow to finish it off. Add three lines on each side of my head as cute whiskers.

8. Finally, draw two tiny ovals for eyes, and another to make my nose.

9. Now you've drawn all the important bits, it's time to trace round the edges with a black pen so your picture starts to look more like the real me!

10. Rub out all the extra pencil lines, then decorate my outfit and colour me in.

Tip:
Have fun dressing me up in different outfits. You could use scraps of material or patterned paper to make my dress, sprinkle on some glitter or even use sparkly beads and sequins for a party look. I make a fabulous model for all budding fashion designers!

Now try drawing Mimmy.
My twin sister Mimmy looks just like me, except she wears her hair-bow on the opposite side. That's how people tell us apart!

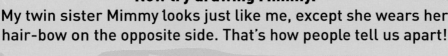

Just dance

Dancing is a brilliant hobby, and it helps you stay healthy, too. I'm always first on the dancefloor at parties, and I love trying out different types of dancing whenever I get the chance. It doesn't matter how good you are, it's just fun to have a go!

Line dancing

Yee-haw! Line-dancing makes me feel like the coolest cowgirl around. The steps aren't too difficult to learn, and someone shouts them out as you're dancing, so it's easy to keep up.
Dress up in: Cute gingham checks, denim and cowboy boots – awesome!

Disco

Disco music is completely fabulous! It's easy to practise routines at home in your bedroom with your favourite music playing. My friends and I especially like disco dancing at parties.
Dress up in: Legwarmers, tights and a sparkly headband – groovy!

Ballroom

There are so many different ballroom dances, it's hard to pick a favourite. I like the jive and the waltz best. I love practising at home with Mimmy. She's a very graceful dancer.
Dress up in: Twirly, sparkly, sequin-covered dresses and strappy sandals – I'm in glitter-ball heaven!

Tap

Tap dancing makes me feel like an old-fashioned movie star. I'm always trying out new steps at home, or toe-tapping and heel-clicking around the kitchen! It's noisy but so exciting, and I love dancing along to fabulous show-tunes.
Dress up in: Leggings, a leotard and (of course) some fancy tap-shoes – totally showbiz!

Ballet

I've been going to ballet classes for a while now. I love everything about it, from the amazing classical music to the graceful steps and movements. Don't be fooled – it might look beautiful, but it takes loads of hard work and effort, too!
Dress up in: Pastel-coloured leotards, tutus and ballet slippers – so pretty.

Street dance

Don't let the name confuse you – street dancing happens indoors, as well as outside! It's sometimes called hip-hop dancing, and is fast, furious and totally cool! My friends and I make a great crew and love challenging each other to dance-offs.
Dress up in: Baggy trousers, trainers and a cute T-shirt – be street smart!

Story starters

Writing is one of my favourite hobbies, and I love making up stories! Have a go at one of your own, using a few of my favourite tips to get you started.

Ready, steady, start

Finding a brilliant beginning can sometimes be the hardest part of writing a story. Try starting with this if you're stuck:

Dear Daniel was especially good at three things.

Number one: *taking brilliant photographs.*

Number two: ....
....

And number three: ....
....

Fill in the gaps, and then carry on with the rest of the story!

Or use one of these starting sentences instead:
* When Princess Hello Kitty woke up, there was a strange noise coming from outside the castle.
* One miserable March morning, Rory made a massive mistake.
* Fifi's dad was always, always late, and it drove her bonkers.
* 'I just don't understand it,' cried Grandma. 'Why on earth would someone want to steal my carpet slippers?'
* Thomas and Tracy were both learning to play the guitar.

16

Terrific titles

A title tells you what to expect from a book, and they can give you plenty of good story ideas, too. See if you can write one to go with each of these titles.

★ *The Invisible Pony*
★ *Fifi and the Cupcake Fairies*
★ *Introducing Flora Fancypants*
★ *Puppies in Space*
★ *Hello Kitty and the Pirates*
★ *The Mystery of the Missing Tiara*

Get in character

Lots of the best stories have a main character, with a problem that needs to be solved. It could be a big problem or a small one – that's up to the writer (you!). Fill in this handy list to get your story going.

Character's name: ....
....

Description: ....
....
....

The story takes place in: ....
....
....

The character's friends are: ....
....
....

The character's problem is: ....
....
....

Now, work out how your character is going to solve the problem, and get writing!

Space Kitty

Three, two, one... blast off! Can you spot ten differences between these two pictures? Circle them all on the opposite page.

How does your garden grow?

I love having my own little patch of garden! Mama and Papa let me plant whatever I like, and it's so much fun watching my flowers, herbs, fruit and veggies grow.

Home grown

Hey, green fingers! Why not have a go at growing some of my favourites? If you don't have a garden, lots of them will grow in pots on a patio or windowsill, too!

Strawberries

I could scoff strawberries all day long! Instead of planting seeds, we bought some really small strawberry plants, and put them in the ground. They've grown loads since then – it's amazing! In the spring, they had pretty white flowers before the strawberries came along.

Did you know?
Strawberries are green and really small to begin with. They grow, and then slowly turn from green to red!

Herbs

In the summer, I grow herbs in the garden. Then, when the weather gets cold, we keep them in a pot on the windowsill instead. My favourites are rosemary, basil and oregano. They smell amazing, and I love chopping them up to sprinkle over homemade pizzas.

Flowers

It was so hard choosing which flowers to grow, because they're all so beautiful. In the end, these are the ones I went for.

★ **Pansies** are easy to grow and last for ages. The flowers also look like they've got tiny little faces in the middle, which is SO cute!

★ **Roses** are much taller and grander than pansies. I'm always careful around their prickly stems, but they smell totally gorgeous.

★ **Nasturtiums** (say nuh-ster-shums) are bright, bold and very cheerful.

★ **Sunflowers** are famous for their size. Last year, one of mine ended up being taller than Papa!

★ **Daisies** grow all over our lawn! I love picking them and making them into daisy chain necklaces, bracelets and crowns.

Cress

Cress is one of the fastest and easiest things for any gardener to grow. Instead of planting seeds in the ground, I put them in little pots. If you paint a face on the side of the pot, when the cress starts to grow it looks like curly green hair!

Stage struck

I love putting on shows with my friends! Whether it's a play or a concert, we always have a brilliant time. Everyone's good at different things, so we all help out in different ways. Check out my top tips for staging a show of your own. Encore!

Where to stage it

You don't actually need a stage to put on a show. As long as you've got some space for performing and room for an audience to sit and watch, almost anywhere will do! In winter, it might be your living room and in summer, the garden or your local park are perfect.

Dressing up

Costumes really help to set the mood for your play. It's often easy to take clothes from your own wardrobe (or someone else's!) and mix them together to get the perfect look. For instance, if your play is set in the past, ask your grandma if she's got any old clothes you could borrow. Think about recycling things from around the house, too. Old sheets and pillowcases are perfect for sewing or pinning together to make brand new costumes!

Play away

A play tells a story, just like a film or TV show. It can be funny or serious, magical or realistic and can also include singing and dancing. Depending on the story, you might need lots of actors, or just one or two. Sometimes, it's possible for one person to dress up as more than one character in the same play! You can borrow plays (or scripts) from your local library, but it's even more fun to write your own. Try making up the plot as you go along, or base it on a story you already know. (I love turning my favourite books into mini-plays to act out with my friends!)

Setting the scene

A set is the background for your stage, and your story. My favourite way of making a set when I'm putting on a play in the garden is to use cardboard boxes. You can pile them up, and then paint anything you want on the sides. If your play is set in a town or city, they might look like buildings, or you could paint on trees and flowers for a country scene. Indoors, try using an old sheet instead. You can paint on it in just the same way, and then hang it from a curtain pole or clothes rail.

Did you know?
A story with songs is usually called a musical, instead of a play.

Tickets and posters

To let the audience know about your play, you could draw a cool poster. Make sure you include the name of the play, who's going to star in it, and when it's happening. You could use smaller pieces of paper as tickets, too!

The audience

So, now you're ready to perform, who's going to watch you? Invite as many people as you've got room for – your family, friends and maybe some neighbours, too. If there's not enough space for everyone, you might have to do two performances!

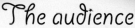

Opening night!

Accessorise!

Accessorising is a skill every good fashionista needs. See if you can match the perfect accessory to each of these outfits.

1.

3.

4.

5.

6.

8.

9.

10.

11.

Accessories

Boredom busters!

Next time you can't think of anything to do, I've got the answer.
Pick out one of these silly-but-fun activities and
use it to give your boredom the boot!

How it works

Close your eyes and turn this book around three times.
Keeping your eyes shut, drop your finger down to point
at one of the suggestions. The activities on the left side
of the page are all things you can do on your own. The
ones on the right are best if you're with a friend (or a
few). If your finger doesn't land exactly on one of the
ideas, pick the one that's nearest. Now, give it a try!

☆ On your own ★

2. Learn a magic trick (find a library book or website to help you).

3. Make up your own board game.

1. Start a scrapbook, using words, photos, stickers and pretty paper.

4. Make a crown and wear it all day. Ask people to call you 'Your Highness'.

5. Rearrange your books in colour order, so your shelves look like a rainbow.

7. Try to break a world record.

6. Pretend you're a rock star, and practise singing into your hairbrush in front of the mirror.

8. Learn to balance a spoon on your nose.

9. Talk like a pirate for an hour.

10. Draw and colour in a map of your bedroom, house or street.

Fun with friends

1. Have a dance-off to see who can make up the craziest moves.

2. Invent a secret code and use it to write messages to each other.

3. Plan what the world would be like if you were all jointly in charge.

4. Pretend you're supermodels and set up a fun photo-shoot.

5. Play pop star charades. Choose a pop star. Don't tell anyone else who they are and mime their actions. Whoever guesses the correct answer first is the winner.

6. Make a den using chairs and blankets. Ask if you can eat your lunch inside.

7. Draw cartoon pictures of each other.

8. Dream up some silly acts and start your own circus.

9. Make each other friendship bracelets.

10. Make sock puppets and stage a puppet play.

27

Stylish stationery

From pretty pens and pencils to totally adorable notebooks, I'm crazy about cute stationery. It's perfect for brightening up your desk, and it helps make homework more fun, too! Check out these crafty ideas for giving plain pieces of stationery a fabulous new look.

One of a kind
I love making my own stationery. You get one-of-a-kind designs and make your pocket money go a bit further. Genius!

Gift-wrapped and gorgeous
Save the wrapping from special birthday presents or parcels and use it to decorate your stationery. Fancy patterned paper, ribbons and bows are all perfect for the job!

Dots and spots
Dip the eraser on the end of a new pencil into some paint. Press it down on to a plain notebook or pencil case, to make a neat dot. Do this lots of times to build up a cute, spotty pattern all over.

Hello Kitty's most glittery notebook

Pretty patterns

Take a notebook and open it out flat. Lay it on top of some fabric or patterned paper. Cut out a rectangle that's a bit bigger than the notebook. Spread glue all over the outside of the notebook and press the fabric or paper on top. Fold over the edges and stick them inside for a neat and tidy finish.

Shimmer shapes

Pick a nice bold shape like a heart, star or flower, and draw it on to the front of a notebook. Fill in the whole shape with a thin layer of white glue. Sprinkle glitter or sequins all over the glue. Leave to dry, and then shake off any excess sparkly stuff. Shiny, huh?!

Hello Kitty's prettiest notebook

Tip: You could try the same idea on a fabric pencil case.

Younger Hello Kitty fans should always ask an adult to help them before using scissors or anything sharp.

Sparkles and ladders

This fun board game is played in the same way as Snakes and Ladders—it's just more stylish! Instead of snakes there are sparkly necklaces, and I've decorated the ladders with a few of my favourite bows.

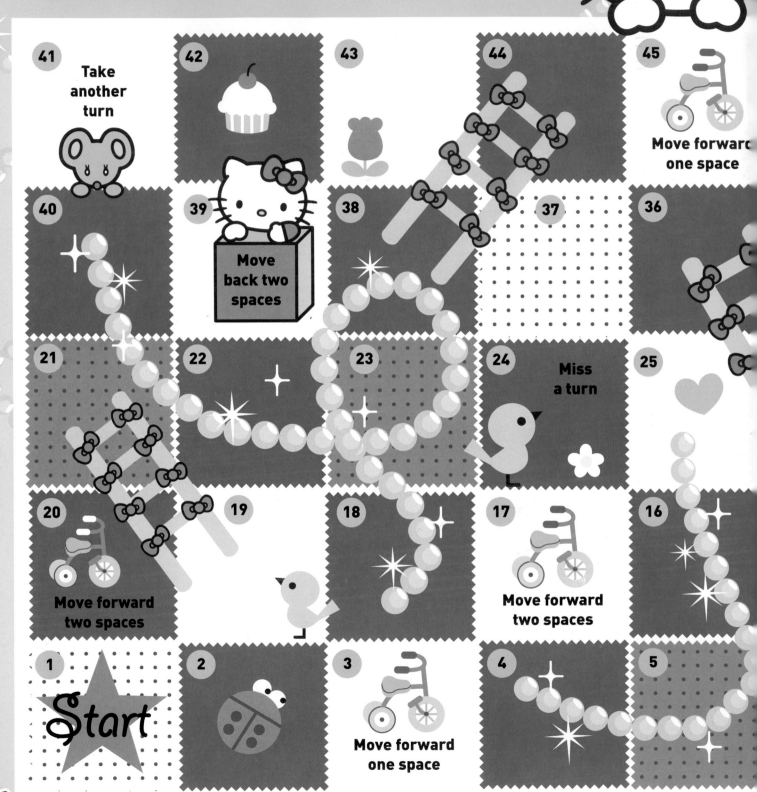

41 Take another turn

42

43

44

45 Move forward one space

40

39 Move back two spaces

38

37

36

21

22

23

24 Miss a turn

25

20 Move forward two spaces

19

18

17 Move forward two spaces

16

1 Start

2

3 Move forward one space

4

5

30

You will need:

★ Buttons, counters or circles of coloured card
★ A die
Tip: So you know which is your counter, make sure all the buttons or circles of card are a different colour.

How to play:
Each player chooses a different button, counter or circle of card and places it on the 'start' square. Take it in turns to throw the die and move the number of spaces it shows.
★ If you land on a sparkly necklace, slide down it to the bottom. ★ Landed on a ladder square? Hurrah! Climb up to the top. ★ Follow any instructions on the other squares when you land on them. The first person to make it to the end of the game is the winner!

47

48 **Move back two spaces**

49

50 **Win!**

34

33 **Take another turn**

32

31

26

27

28 **Move back one space**

29

30

14

13

12

11 **Miss a turn**

7

8 **Move back one space**

9

10

Time capsule

A time capsule is a special record of your life. It's fun to put together, and even more fun – one day in the future – to open it up and see how much you've changed!

Why?

I love it when Mama gets out baby photos of me and Mimmy! We were so cute and it's amazing to see how different we looked when we were younger. A time capsule is even better because it contains lots more information than a box of photos.

Who?

Your time capsule is all about you and your life, so it's completely up to you what you put inside. I've made a list of ideas to get you started.

★ **Photos** – recent pics of you, your family, friends and pets. You could also include photos of your bedroom, your house, your street or your school.

★ **Magazines** – when you've finished reading the newest issue of your favourite magazine or comic, drop it into the capsule.

★ **Questionnaire** – copy out the questions on the opposite page along with your answers.

★ **Friends** – to make a record of your best pals, ask them each to write a special message for you to include.

★ **Wrappers** – have you bought anything this week? Add the wrappers or tags to your time capsule, as a record of how you spent your pocket money.

★ **TV guide** – add the TV guide from last week (or print one from the internet), and circle your favourite shows.

What?

When I made my time capsule, I put everything inside an old biscuit tin. Mimmy used a plastic box with a lid for hers. As long as it's clean, dry and can be sealed shut, almost anything will do! If you're planning to hide your time capsule outdoors (in a shed, for instance), it's a good idea to make sure it's waterproof, too.

Where?

Once you've made your time capsule, hide it or ask someone to hide it for you. (If you don't know where it is, you can't get it out and peep at what's inside too soon! But do make sure that they make a note of where the capsule is hidden!) Attics, garden sheds, garages, wardrobes, and the dusty tops of kitchen cupboards all make especially good hiding spots.

When?

It's up to you how long you keep your time capsule hidden. I'm planning to leave mine for at least a year. The longer it's hidden, the more chance you'll have forgotten what's inside, so opening it will be an even better surprise!

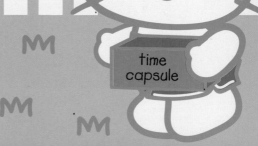

time capsule

Time capsule questionnaire

Copy this out, fill in your answers and add it to your time capsule.

Name: ....

Age: ....

Address: ....

....

Height: ....

Shoe size: ....

Best friends: ....

....

....

Favourite outfit: ....

Favourite film: ....

Favourite book: ....

School: ....

Teacher: ....

Favourite school subject: ....

Least favourite subject: ....

Dream holiday: ....

Three things that make me smile: ....

....

....

My biggest secret: ....

Today I'm wearing: ....

The last thing I bought was: ....

At the weekends I like to: ....

The TV show I'd most like to star in is: ....

My favourite song to dance to is: ....

If I could have any super power it would be: ....

33

How to be a fabulous friend

Everyone loves having lots of friends. Mine are amazing, and I bet yours are, too. Sneak a peek at my favourite tips on being a totally marvellous mate!

Share and share alike

Whether you've had some really good news, or are feeling down in the dumps, be sure to tell your friends. They can celebrate happy times with you, and cheer you up when you're feeling gloomy.

Show you care

A good friend is always kind! If your pal is finding something tricky at school, offer to give her a hand. When she needs some extra practice to make a sports team or win a place in the school choir, join in so she's not doing it on her own. The brilliant thing about true friends is that they'll do the same when you're in a tough spot!

Tip: A good friend knows your secrets, but never, ever shares them with anyone else!

Have fun

Go on - get giggly! Having fun together is one of the best things about being friends. Find out what makes each other smile or laugh, and do lots of it. Whether it's silly jokes, singing at the top of your voices, or visiting the swings in the park, everything is more fun with friends!

Opposites attract

Your friends don't have to be exactly like you; in fact it's sometimes great if they're not! Finding out about what makes your friend different can be brilliant fun. If you both have different hobbies, give her favourites a try and see what they're like. Then, the next time, show her the things you enjoy doing. You're bound to have at least a few things in common.

Say sorry

Everyone has arguments sometimes. If you fall out with a pal, try to talk about the problem, and say sorry afterwards. Sort it out as soon as you can, and maybe do something extra-kind for her to show there are no hard feelings.

Old and new

It's always exciting to make new friends, but it doesn't mean you should forget about your old ones. Invite everyone - old and new - to your house so they can have fun getting to know each other. Most people have a few very special or close pals, but generally when it comes to friends, you can't have too many!

Party pictures

I've been collecting useful things from all around the house, ready for a special birthday party!

Write out the name of each object in the boxes below, then read the letters in the coloured boxes to spell out the name of the person who's celebrating.

1. ☐ r e s s

2. ☐ ☐ ☐ ☐ ☐

3. ☐ ☐ ☐ ☐ ☐ ☐ ☐

4. ☐ ☐ ☐ ☐ ☐

5. c a r d

6. ☐ ☐ ☐ ☐ ☐ ☐ ☐

7. ☐ ☐ ☐ ☐ ☐ ☐ ☐ ☐

8. ☐ ☐ ☐ ☐ ☐ ☐

9. a p p l ☐ s

10. f ☐ o w e r s

The person who's celebrating is:

1   2   3   4   5   6   7   8   9   10

37

What's your superstar style?

Have you ever dreamed of being super-famous?
Take this fun quiz and find out which
superstar job is perfect for you!

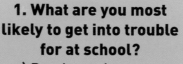

**1. What are you most
likely to get into trouble
for at school?**
a) Daydreaming.
b) Not wearing your
uniform.
c) Talking in class.
d) Showing off.

**2. Which of these
gadgets is your favourite?**
a) MP3 player.
b) Hairdryer.
c) Phone.
d) Television.

**4. What's your favourite
thing about parties?**
a) Rocking out to the
karaoke machine.
b) Giving each other
fabulous makeovers.
c) Playing silly-but-fun
games.
d) Going along in
fancy dress.

**3. One of your friends is down
in the dumps. How would you
cheer her up?**
a) Make a playlist of all her favourite songs.
b) Go out shopping together for a new outfit.
c) Have a good chat and tell her a few jokes.
d) Take over a pile of DVDs and watch some
cool films together.

**5. What's the first thing you do when you
get home from school each day?**
a) Play music.
b) Change your outfit.
c) Chat to your family about your day.
d) Turn on the TV to watch your favourite
programme.

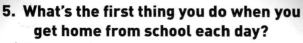

Mostly a)s

You'd make an awesome rock star! You're cool, clever and crazy about music. Tune up, turn on and go for it!

Mostly b)s

You'd make a fabulous supermodel! You're girly, gorgeous and totally fashionable. Put on your favourite outfit and strike a pose!

Results

Mostly c)s

You'd make a brilliant TV presenter! You're fun, friendly and a total chatterbox. Get set to be a small-screen sensation!

Mostly d)s

You'd make an amazing actress! You're confident, funny and love showing off! Lights, camera, rehearsals, action!

Cool colours

Do you always stick to the same shades when you're choosing a new outfit? Does mixing and matching colours put you off painting? Well, you've come to the right girl for help! Read through my rainbow of top tips, and you'll be colour confident in no time at all.

So clever!

The colour wheel

I always use a colour wheel to help out when I'm mixing paint colours. It's made up of the three primary colours – red, blue and yellow. The shades in between are made by mixing together the colours on either side.

Blue + yellow = green   Yellow + red = orange

Red + blue = purple

The white stuff

When you're mixing paint, add some white to make lighter shades of each colour. For instance:

Red + white = pink

Purple + white = lilac

The more white you add, the lighter the colour will be!

40

Colour moods

Colours don't just make things look pretty.
They can make a difference to the way you feel, too.

RED can make
you feel lively and
adventurous.

ORANGE can make
you feel warm
and cosy.

YELLOW can make
you feel sunny
and cheerful.

GREEN can make
you feel in touch
with nature.

BLUE can make
you feel cool
and calm.

PURPLE can
make you feel
bold.

PINK can make
you feel peaceful
and girly.

Stylish shades

When it comes to fashion, I love
mixing and matching all kinds of
colours. These are a few of my
favourites. See if you can find
some similar colour combos
in your wardrobe, or make
up a few of your own!

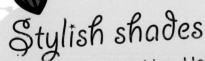

Mega-crossword

Grab a pen, put on your cutest thinking cap and see if you can solve the clues below!

Across

1. I love dancing to _ _ _ _ _ and playing it on my guitar, too. (5)
3. I always wear a cute _ _ _ in my hair. (3)
5. One day, I'd love to be a rich and famous movie _ _ _ _! (4)
7. My _ _ _ _ _ is married to my Papa. (4)
8. The daughter of a king and queen is called a _ _ _ _ _ _ _ _ . (8)
11. I love hanging out with my family and _ _ _ _ _ _ _ . (7)
12. As a treat, I often have a glass of milk and a chocolate-chip _ _ _ _ _ _ . (6)
14. The best thing about Halloween is wearing _ _ _ _ _ dress! (5)
17. When it's my friends' birthdays I love being invited to their _ _ _ _ _ _ _ . (7)
19. _ _ _ _ _ _ is my home city (and the capital of England). (6)
22. I always carry a cute and useful _ _ _ when I go shopping. (3)
23. Wearing a sparkly crown or _ _ _ _ _ makes me feel like royalty! (5)
24. I love putting up the _ _ _ _ _ _ _ _ _ tree and singing carols in December! (9)
25. When the weather is wet, I love trying to spot a _ _ _ _ _ bow between the clouds. (4)
26. The _ _ _ _ _ _ _ _ pool is one of my favourite places, especially in summer. (8)

Down

1. My twin sister is called _ _ _ _ _ _ . (5)
2. My favourite season is _ _ _ _ _ _ _ , because it's warm and sunny. (6)
3. I usually celebrate my _ _ _ _ _ _ _ _ _ with cards, presents and balloons. (8)
4. Wizards and fairies wave a magic _ _ _ _ to cast spells. (4)
5. Midnight feasts, pillow fights and spooky stories are the best things about a _ _ _ _ _ _ _ _ _ . (9)
6. I love getting a _ _ _ _ _ _ _ in the post, especially if it's from one of my friends. (6)
9. Mixing yellow and blue together makes _ _ _ _ _ _ . (5)
10. I have the cutest outfit to go ice- _ _ _ _ _ _ _ _ at the local rink, or roller- _ _ _ _ _ _ _ _ in the park. (7)
13. Tasty _ _ _ cakes are one of my favourite things to bake! (3)
14. Going bowling with my friends is lots of _ _ _ . (3)
15. When we go to the fair, my favourite sweet treat is fluffy pink _ _ _ _ _ floss. (5)
16. To make your paintings sparkle, sprinkle on lots of _ _ _ _ _ _ _ _ ! (7)
18. I love going to the _ _ _ _ _ to spend my pocket money on cute new things. (5)
20. _ _ _ _ Daniel is the kindest boy I know. (4)
21. _ _ _ _ _ _ berries are one of my favourite fruits! (5)

1. 2. 3. 4. 5.

6.

7. 8.

9.

10.

11. 12.

13.

14. 15.

16. 17. 18.

19. 20.

21. 22.

23. 24.

25. 26.

Hopscotch

Hopscotch has been a popular playground game for hundreds of years. You can play it on your own, but it's even more fun if you team up with your friends and turn it into a competition. Pick one of the grids below, grab some chalk and get hopping!

What to do:

Copy one of the grids on to the ground using chalk. You can do this on a playground, pavement or patio, but make sure you ask permission first. Stand at the start of the grid, and take a long stride away from it. Draw a chalk line just in front of your feet. This is your start line.

You will need:

★ Chalk
★ A flat stone, a coin or a small beanbag to use as your marker

The rules:

★ If you step on any of the grid lines when you're hopping, your turn ends and you have to play that number again the next time.

★ If you lose your balance and put down more than one foot (or a hand) inside the same box, your turn ends in the same way.

How to play:

1 Stand behind the start line and throw your marker into the first box. If it misses the box or lands on a different one, you lose your turn. Move on to the next player! If it lands inside the box, you can start hopping. Make your way up the grid, turn round in the 'home' box, then come back to the start. Stop in box number one to pick up your marker, and land back behind the starting line.

2 When you've completed box number one, throw your marker into box two and start again. Keep playing in number order. Your turn is only over when your throw misses a box, or if you make a mistake as you're hopping (see *The rules*).

3 When your turn is over, move on to the next player. Take it in turns to throw and hop your way around the grid. After everyone has had a turn, the first player carries on from where her last try ended. For instance, if you completed boxes one and two, but missed as you threw the marker towards box three, you need to try box three again.

4 The winner is the first person to throw the marker and hop the grid for all the boxes in order.

Wet weather wonder

When it's too wet for outdoor hopscotch, try setting up an indoor version instead. Ask if you can have an old white bed sheet or piece of material, then draw your grid on top with a marker pen. Spread it out on a carpet (never a wooden or tiled floor), and you're ready to play!

The classic

This grid mixes up hopping and jumping. You hop the single boxes (three, six and nine) on one foot, but jump on those which are side by side. For example, for boxes four and five on the way up the grid, jump with your left foot on number four and your right foot on number five.

The snail

In this grid, every box is hopped. You hop into each section on the same leg as you go round the grid. When you reach the 'home' box, you can swap legs if you want to, but you must then hop back to the start on that same leg. Go on – you can do it!

45

Fairground fun

Big top

Mimmy and I are having fun at the fair! We're trying to find our way from the big top to the candy floss stand. Can you help us get there, without stopping off at the Ferris Wheel or the ice-cream stand?

Start

Ferris wheel

Ice cream

Finish

Candy floss

47

Kitty cupcakes

Have a go at baking some of these cute cupcakes for a party, or as a special treat. I borrowed the recipe from my grandma, and it's super-delicious!

Always ask a grown-up to help you in the kitchen!

You will need:

For the cupcakes:
- ★ 125g soft butter
- ★ 125g caster sugar
- ★ 2 eggs
- ★ 125g self-raising flour
- ★ 1 tablespoon milk
- ★ A large mixing bowl
- ★ A wooden spoon
- ★ A small bowl
- ★ A cupcake tray or muffin tin
- ★ Cupcake cases

For the frosting:
- ★ 100g soft butter
- ★ 100g icing sugar

What to do:

1. Ask your grown-up helper to turn the oven on to 190ºC (370ºF / Gas Mark 5).
2. Put the butter and sugar into a large bowl. Stir hard until they're completely mixed together.
3. Break the eggs into a smaller bowl, then tip them into the butter and sugar mixture.
4. Add the flour and the tablespoon of milk. Stir everything together to make a nice, smooth cake mixture.
5. Check the *Fabulous flavours* list opposite, and stir in any extra ingredients.
6. Line each section of your cupcake tray with a paper case. Add a spoonful of the cake mixture to each case, so it's roughly half full.
7. Ask your grown-up to put your cakes in the oven for 15-20 minutes. They should be springy and golden brown on top when they're done.
8. Ask your grown-up helper to take the cakes out of the oven when they are ready. Allow the cakes to cool while you make some yummy frosting. Stir the butter and icing sugar together in a large bowl, until they're smooth and creamy. Mix in any flavourings.
9. When the cakes are completely cool, spread a little bit of frosting on top of each one. Decorate with sprinkles or slices of tasty fresh fruit!

Fabulous flavours

Choose one of these yummy flavour combinations to make your cakes even tastier.

Bananarama
✷ Add 50g chocolate chips or raisins to the cake mixture.
✷ Add half a mashed banana to the frosting.
✷ Decorate with dried banana chips or chocolate sprinkles.

Yummy!

Go fruity
✷ Add 2 teaspoons of raspberry jam to the frosting.
✷ Decorate with chopped fruit.

Vanilla strawberry
✷ Add 1 teaspoon of vanilla essence to the cake mixture.
✷ Add 6 mashed strawberries to the frosting.
✷ Decorate with strawberry slices or pink sprinkles.

Don't forget to wash your hands before you start baking. I usually wear an apron, too – it looks cute and stops the rest of my outfit getting messy.

Perfect perfume

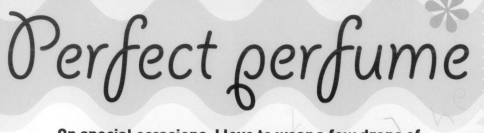

On special occasions, I love to wear a few drops of pretty-smelling perfume. Mimmy and I often make our own using rose petals from the garden. If you want to try it out for yourself, here's our secret recipe!

You will need:
- ★ 3-4 roses
- ★ 2 jugs
- ★ Hot water
- ★ A small bottle with a lid
- ★ Art supplies for decorating
- ★ A funnel (optional)
- ★ A sieve

Never pick roses without asking permission first!

What to do:
1. Pull the petals off your roses, and put them into a large jug.
2. Ask a grown-up to cover them with very hot water. Leave the petals to soak in the water for at least two hours. Make sure that the water is cool before you go on to step 3.
3. Pour the mixture through a sieve into a second jug. Squeeze the petals between your fingers to get out as much perfume as you can.
4. Carefully pour the perfumed water into a bottle. (Use a funnel if you can – it will make this part much easier.)
5. Put the lid on, then add a label and decorate your bottle.

Tip: If there's too much perfume for one bottle, why not fill up a few extras so your friends can enjoy it, too?

Finishing touches

Try one of these cute ideas to make your bottle look extra-gorgeous.

★ Tie a piece of sparkly ribbon in a bow around the top of the bottle.

★ Print off a label, using your favourite fancy computer font. Wrap some pretty paper around the middle of the bottle, and add the label on top.

★ Write the name of your perfume on to plain paper and stick to the front of the bottle. Glue sparkly sequins or tiny flowers all around the edges.

★ Cut out a rose shape from red or pink felt, and some green felt leaves. Glue them to the front of the bottle.

Hello Kitty's Perfect Perfume

Where to wear
Put a little bit of your rose perfume on each wrist and some more just behind your ears. Don't wear too much – as all stylish girls know, less is more!

A rose by any other name
Most fancy perfumes have a fancy name to match. These are some of my ideas:
★ Kitty Rose
★ Blush
★ Pretty Posy
★ Rosa
★ Petalicious
★ Bloom
See if you can come up with some more of your own!

Bathing beauty

Add a few spoonfuls of rose-petal perfume to your bath water for extra-soft, yummy-smelling skin.

Words and pictures
Hannah FATH

Puzzles are so much fun! See how many of these words you can find hidden in the letter square. Draw a ring around each one when you spot it, and put a tick next to the picture clue, too.

Balloon

Rainbow

Books

Bow

Apple

Boat

Elephant

Present

Flower

Guitar

Butterfly

House

Crown

Shoes

Bird

Star

Heart

Bee

Cake

Clock

Letter

Teddy

Car

Dress

Camera

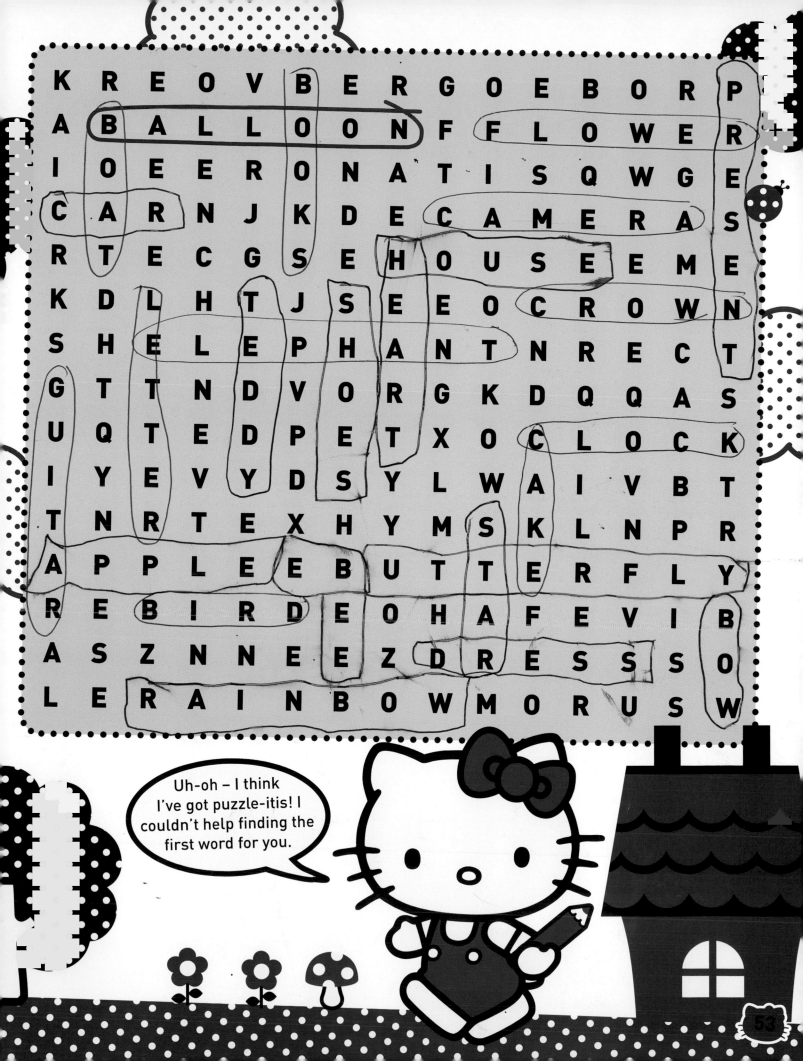

K R E O V B E R G O E B O R P

A B A L L O O N F F L O W E R E

I I O E E R O N A T I S Q W G R

C C A R N J K D E C A M E R A S

R R T E C G S E H O U S E E M E

K K D L H T J S E E O C R O W N

S S H E L E P H A N T N R E C T

G G T T N D V O R G K D Q Q A S

U U Q T E D P E T X O C L O C K

I I Y Y E V V Y D S Y L W A I V B T

T T N R T E X H Y M S K L N P R

A A P P L E E B U T T E R F L Y

R R E B I R D E O H A F E V I B

A A S Z N N E E Z D R E S S S O

L L E R A I N B O W M O R U S W

Uh-oh – I think I've got puzzle-itis! I couldn't help finding the first word for you.

Hello bingo

Have you ever played Bingo before? It's one of my favourite games, especially on a rainy day indoors with Mimmy or my friends. I've invented a fun new version featuring some of my favourite things (and some super-cute costumes!), so you can have a go, too.

You will need:

- ★ Scrap paper
- ★ A pen or pencil
- ★ Scissors
- ★ A bowl
- ★ Coins or buttons

Younger Hello Kitty fans should always ask an adult before using scissors.

Before you start:

- ★ Copy all the words in this list on to some scrap paper.
- ★ Cut the paper into strips, so there's one word on each piece.
- ★ Fold the paper strips in half and put them in a bowl.

Anchor	Cookies	Music
Angel	Crocodile	Necklace
Artist	Crown	Penguin
Astronaut	Dolphin	Plane
Ballerina	Flowers	Popcorn
Bath	Frog	Pumpkin
Bell	Handbag	Rocket
Boat	Hat	Rock star
Bunny	Horse	Sailor
Car	House	Shells
Cheerleader	Ice cream	Shooting star
Chef	Jam	Strawberry
Cherries	Leaves	Sun
Chick	Lion	Telephone
Clown	Mimmy	Twins
Comb	Mushrooms	Umbrella

How to play:

- ★ Pick someone to be the caller for the first round of the game.
- ★ Ask everyone else to choose a bingo card (the caller doesn't need one).
- ★ There are four cards on the opposite page, separated by the dotted lines. You can either play on the page opposite, copy the cards on to separate pieces of paper, or ask a grown-up to photocopy the cards for you instead.
- ★ If you're the caller, take one of the paper strips out of the bowl and read out the word.
- ★ If you're a player, check your card to see if the word matches one of the pictures on your card. Place a coin or button over that picture or cross it off with a pen. (You don't need to do anything if it doesn't match any of the pictures on your card.)
- ★ Keep playing in the same way, reading out one word at a time.
- ★ The first person to cover up all of their pictures, shouts 'bingo!' and is the winner.

Tip: Choose a different person to be the caller for each round of the game. That way, everyone gets an equal chance to play and (most importantly) win!

Princess Ball

Why throw a plain and simple party, when you can host a royal ball instead? Dress up in your most fabulous outfit and prepare to party like a princess!

Tip: To get into the spirit of things, call your party venue the ballroom and your outfit, your ball-gown!

You're invited

Set the tone for your princess ball when you send out the invitations. Keep them smart, simple and pretty, with just a little bit of sparkle for added glamour. I love the idea of decorating them with little crowns, and – of course – including your royal seal when you close the envelope!

Is it a ball or a party?

As long as there's dancing and everyone dresses smartly, you can definitely call it a ball. It's really just a grand word for a dance party!

Holes made a either edge

Crown shapes cut from thin card

Younger Hello Kitty fans should always ask an adult before using scissors.

Dear Dear Daniel,
You are invited to my fabulous Princess Ball.
Dress code: Princesses and Prince Charming.
Love Princess Hello Kitty xx

Fabulous food

Try serving these stylish-but-delicious snacks to your guests.
★ Dainty finger sandwiches
★ Tasty dips with breadsticks or raw veggies
★ Tiny pizzas (cut out the dough with a cookie cutter!)
★ Heart-shaped cookies
★ Chocolate-frosted fairy cakes
★ A yummy fresh fruit platter
And to drink? Crush some raspberries and add them to a jug of lemonade, for a pink drink that's princess-y perfection!

Always ask an adult to elp you in the kitchen.

Tip-top tiaras

To make sure everyone feels perfectly princess-ish, why not make your own sparkly tiaras? It's the perfect party activity! Ask everyone to bring along a plain hair band, then have fun decorating them with shiny pipe-cleaners, beads and sequins. They'll make the perfect finishing touch to your ball-gown as you twirl around the dance floor!

String or ribbon threaded though

Royal decorations

Draw lots of crown shapes on to thin pieces of card and cut them out. Make holes in the points at each side, then thread them on to string to make a fabulous royal garland. Hang up as many as you like, and add some pretty balloons, too.
Tip: Your crown garlands will look even better if you decorate them with patterned paper, glitter, scraps of fabric or sparkly sequins.

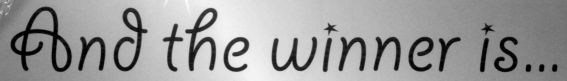

And the winner is...

Sssh! Don't tell anyone, but I secretly love watching award shows on the TV. From the glamorous outfits and the shiny trophies to the silly speeches, they're just fabulous! But you don't need to be a superstar to be a winner – write the name of someone you know on each of these special awards.

The Kitties

The most famous acting awards are the Oscars. I think I'd call my award ceremony 'the Kitties'. What would you call yours?

Awarded to

Ruby + Ella

for being the most brilliant friend ever!

Awarded to

mummy

for making me laugh more than anyone else in the world!

Awarded to

....

for being the person most likely
to save the planet

Awarded to

....

for being the kindest and most
helpful person I know!

Awarded to

Hannon cavin

for having a fabulous singing voice!

Awarded to

....

for being a total sporting genius!

Awarded to

mummy

for baking the yummiest food
I've ever tasted!

Awarded to

....

for making up the craziest
dance routines ever!

Goodbye!

I really hope you've enjoyed reading my Annual. Don't forget to check back for ideas and fun things to do all through the year. Have lots of fun in 2013, whatever you get up to. I'm planning to make it the best year ever!

Love,

Hello Kitty

x x

Answers

Pages 18-19
Space Kitty

Pages 46-47
Fairground fun!

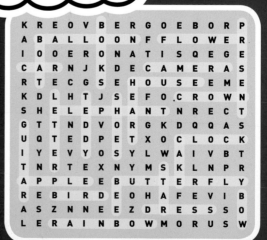

Pages 24-25
Accessorise!

1. d **2.** i **3.** g **4.** b
5. a **6.** c **7.** j **8.** k **9.** h
10. f **11.** e **12.** l

Pages 36-37
Party pictures!

The person who's celebrating is Dear Daniel.

Pages 52-53
Words and pictures

```
K R E O V B E R G O E B O R P
A B A L L O O N F F L O W E R
I O O E R O N A T I S Q E G E
C A R N J K D E C A M E R A S
R T E C G S E H O U S E E M E
K D L H T J S E F O C R O W N
S H E L E P H A N T N R E C T
G T T N D V O R G K D Q Q A S
U Q T E D P E T X O C L O C K
I Y E V V O S Y L W A I V B T
T N R T E X N Y M S K L N P R
A P P L E E B U T T E R F L Y
R E B I R D E O H A F E V I B
A S Z N E E Z D R E S S S O
L E R A I N B O W M O R U S W
```